NICHOLAS [WONG LAI BENG]

An Interpretation of the Way

As Received by an Imperfect Vessel

Copyright © 2021 by Nicholas [Wong Lai Beng]

All rights reserved. No part of this publication may be reproduced, stored or transmitted in any form or by any means, electronic, mechanical, photocopying, recording, scanning, or otherwise without written permission from the publisher. It is illegal to copy this book, post it to a website, or distribute it by any other means without permission.

Nicholas [Wong Lai Beng] asserts the moral right to be identified as the author of this work.

Nicholas [Wong Lai Beng] claims neither ownership nor origination of the ideas contained within these pages. Only the words and their organization are the product of the author through sythesis and reinterpretation through a broad variety of sources.

First edition

This book was professionally typeset on Reedsy. Find out more at reedsy.com

I am like an idiot, my mind is so empty.

- Lao Tzu

Preface

I acknowledge the inherent irony of a book about the indescribable. The Old Master bows to this fact in the opening passage of their great work.

The Dao De Jing (also titled: The Classic of the Way and Its Virtue, The Book of the Way, the Lao Tzu, The Laozi, and the Tao Te Ching among others) was possibly penned by the sage Lao Tzu (Old Boy) or was potentially the product of many hands over centuries. Likewise, its date of composition can be set in the late Spring and Autumn Period or early in the Warring States period at some point between the fifth and sixth centuries BCE. It seems appropriate that questions surrounding a book of timeless mysteries remain equally unanswerable.

Despite the uncertainty of its origin, this collection of poetic sayings is the second most translated book into the English language, surpassed only by the Christian bible. Each translation brings with it the translator's own poetic sensibilities and has its own unique insight and merit. With great variance between them, it is difficult to say that any sort of definitive version exists; indeed, the work you are currently reading certainly does not claim to be one.

In this book, I have attempted to render an interpretation of the Dao De Jing that harmonizes its exquisite imprint on my mind with the honest variety of its many translations. This is not a translation itself, as I am limited to English renditions due to my own inadequacy. Rather, this book is a synthesis of numerous translations into English, more than 10 years in the making.

Like most who come to read the Dao De Jing, the first time I encountered its wisdom was as a child, many years before I would touch its pages:

"A journey of a thousand leagues begins with a single step"

I was a teenager before I picked up the slim book and early into adulthood before I was touched by the beautiful mystery of its verses. By then, I had read several translations of the Dao De Jing. Though I found a common undercurrent running through the often contradictory turns of phrase, I could not match the profound concepts being communicated with the translators' words.

What follows is the summation of one soul's modest studies into the various attempted translations of the Dao De Jing as filtered through the accumulated experiences of the interpreter's life to date. Its intention is to express the Old Master's teachings in the manner as I have received them. We write such poetry to whisper truths that our words cannot contain.

Throughout this interpretation, "The Way" is used in place of Dao or Tao. This is because modern parlance is increasingly developing its use of "The Way" to denote a philosophy or creed at the heart of an individual (or culture) that is in accordance with and identical to the underlying truth of existence. My hope is that this will be more accessible to native English speakers like myself.

To reconcile every divide by living in acceptance of the way things are; to exist simultaneously as the one and the many; to continuously strive for union through the recognition that you are already an essential part of everything; that is the essence of the Dao. When we see beyond the veil of suffering to realize that we are already living in harmony with nature, we are free to accept the privilege of awareness as heaven itself.

If the Dao is the truth underpinning this universe, the Dao De Jing is a record of its comings and goings. It is a direct transmission of an ancient insight, as poignant today as it was when it was written. The fact that I commit these revelations to writing does not indicate any level of attainment on my behalf. To comprehend and, more importantly, to implement The Way in one's own life is an eternal pursuit. By embracing my own incompleteness, may I find completeness; by dwelling in humility, may I remain an imperfect vessel.

This book is an offering of gratitude to the source of all things. Through these words, may you feel my abiding love for you, existing exactly where, when, and as you are.

- Nicholas [Wong Lai Beng]

I

The Classic of Dao

On the nature of existence and the true relation of its parts

1

The Way that can be spoken is not the true Way;
The name that can be named is not the true name.

Without a name, it is the completion of truth;
Given a name, it is mother to ten thousand things.

Desireless, we understand the mystery of the Way;
Bound by desire, we fail to comprehend the obvious.

The Way and the world emerge from the same source:
The mystery within a mystery, the shadow in the dark.

Yet, it alone is the path to wisdom.

2

To know the beautiful, one must comprehend the plain.
To attain the good, one must contend with the evil.

In this way,
Being and absence create each other;
Difficulty and ease produce each other;
Length and shortness depend on each other;
Before and after follow each other.

Thus, the master accomplishes without action
And imparts wisdom without teaching.

What life manifests, they let come;
What life dissipates, they let go;

What the master carries, they do not possess;
Their labour seeks no reward.
Their task complete, it is forgotten.
That is why the master's work lasts forever.

3

To dispel longing, hold no preferences;
To deter thieves, value no possessions;
To maintain order, embody order within.

Therefore, the master completes their task
By emptying their mind and filling the void,
By weakening ambition and fortifying resolve.

Their teaching requires liberation from preconception and desire,
For those who know cannot be taught.

Do without doing: give up judgment and expectation.
WEI WU WEI: exist in harmony with the soul.

4

The Way is like the emptiness of a cup.
It is an endless void containing all possibility;
Its use is inexhaustible.

Hidden but ever present, it resolves all contradictions.

It alone is without origin.

5

The Way has no preferences;
It creates both good and evil.

The master has no preferences;
They minister to saints and sinners.

The Way is like a bellows:
In its emptiness, it is infinite potential;
In its use, it produces without limitation.

The more you speak of it, the less you understand.
Keep to the silence and maintain the centre.

6

Still while in motion,
The Way is the great mother.
Overflowing with nothingness,
It gives birth to all existence.

It dwells in each corner of the temple
And bows to the master at work.

7

The Way is infinite and immortal.
Never born, it shall never die.
Free from the illusion of identity,
There is nowhere it is not.

Therefore, by putting themselves last,
The master occupies the highest place.
Detached from the many,
They are one with the all.
Detached from the self,
All ends are accomplished.

8

The highest excellence is that of water.
Its very presence nourishes all things;
It is content in the low places all despise.
Thus, it follows the Way.

When Living, be humble;
When Thinking, be simple;
When Acting, be virtuous;
When Ruling, be merciful;
When Working, be joyous;
When with Family, be present.

When one is content with their circumstances,
Without comparison or competition,
All of nature will bow to them.

9

Fill a bowl to the brim and it shall spill.
Make a blade too sharp and it shall blunt.
Pursue riches and thieves shall find you.
Seek high esteem and you shall be a slave.

Your tasks complete, withdraw into obscurity.

This is the Way of Heaven.

10

Shepherd the wandering mind
And maintain oneness with origination.
Attend to each breath in turn
And remain supple as a babe.
Remove the veil from your eyes
And receive the pure light of creation.
Love every soul you meet
And do not impose your will.
Allow the river of fate to follow its course
And free yourself from concern.

To create without destruction,
To have without possession,
To act without expectation,
To lead without domination,

This is the limitless virtue of the Way.

11

Thirty spokes are joined in a wheel,
But the centre bore turns the axle.

Shaped clay becomes a pot,
But its emptiness holds the water.

Doorways and walls are erected,
But the space within becomes a home.

When spoken, thoughts acquire being,
But their meaning exists as non-being.

12

Colour blinds the eye;
Sound deafens the ears;
Flavour numbs the tongue;
Thought weakens the mind;
Desire poisons the soul.

The master recognizes the world as illusion.
Liberated from attachment,
Their heart is as open as the sky.

13

Good fortune is as precarious as calamity;
Hope is as evanescent as fear.

When ascending or descending a ladder,
Your position is uncertain.
With two feet on the ground,
Your balance is secure.

The master is free from ambition and despair;
Their feet are set firmly upon the Way.

Hope and fear are shadows of anticipation.
They arise when the individual is perceived as self.
Knowing the self as the all,
What has the master to fear?

Therefore, one who would conquer the world
Must first conquer themself.

Love the world as the self and trust in the Way.

14

We look, but cannot see - for it is beyond form.
We listen, but do not hear - for it is beyond sound.
We reach, but cannot grasp - for it is beyond subtlety.
That which is beyond definition
Embodies the unity of all things.

Above, it is not bright; below, it is not dark.
Free from separation, it is nameless.
It was, is, and will return to nothing.

Form of the formless,
Reflection of the invisible,
Subtle beyond conception,
It remains untouched by thought or word.

Looking back, it has no beginning;
Looking forward, it has no end;
Incomprehensible, it cannot be known,
But it is the source of life itself.

Recognize what you come from.
This is the essence of all wisdom.

15

The masters of old understood the mysteries of the Way.
Their thoughts remain incomprehensibly sublime;
Their great knowledge defies transmission.

Therefore, we know only what they appeared to be:
Careful as one who crosses a winter stream;
Vigilant as a warrior in enemy territory;
Courteous as a guest of a great house;
Impermanent as the morning frost;
Simple as uncarved wood;
Open as the valley;
Clear as muddy water;

Remain patient in stillness and the mud will settle;
Remain unmoved and the moment for action will arrive.

The masters alone do not seek fulfillment.
Not seeking, not expecting, they meet each moment.

16

Empty the mind of every thought
And maintain the centre.

Observe chaos arise out of order
And contemplate its return to source.

Everything that grows returns to its root.
To reclaim the root of being is called stillness;
To attain stillness is called serenity;
To cultivate serenity is called destiny;
To fulfill destiny is called enlightenment.

Thus enlightened, the master has returned to source.

If you do not see your root, you will stumble.
Recognizing its origin,
The soul becomes compassionate.
In its compassion, it is dignified as a crown.
In its dignity, it is immersed in Heaven.

That which is of heaven is of the Way.

Following the Way,
The master bears the burden of the world
And their death shall find them waiting.

17

When the master governs, the citizens are hardly aware.
Next best is a leader who is loved;
Next, one who is feared;
The lowest is a tyrant whom all despise.

Distrust people and you make them untrustworthy.

Unspeaking, the master does what must be done.
When the work is complete, the people will say:
"We have done it for ourselves!"

18

When the great Way is forgotten,
Morality and codes of ethics appear.

When cleverness and cunning are prized,
Hypocrisy and pretense emerge.

When the house shakes in disharmony,
Respect and filial piety arise.

When the state falls into chaos,
Loyal patriots are born.

19

Cast out holiness and sagacity!
The people shall benefit a hundred fold.

Give up cleverness and profit!
The people shall not become thieves.

These judgments are insufficient
And shall weaken the people.

Maintain the centre.
Exhibit the plainness of undyed cloth.

Spare no regard for the self
And make your desires few.

20

Where is the difference between yes and no?
Where is the difference between good and bad?
To fear what all men fear is to drown in their terror.

The multitude are satisfied in their pleasures,
Having feasted on the sacrificial ox.

I alone remain unfulfilled.
Like a newborn, yet to smile,
I appear forlorn; I have no home to return to.

The multitude have all they need;
I alone possess nothing.

I am like an idiot, my mind is so empty.

Ordinary people appear so bright;
I alone am dark.
Other people appear so sharp;
I alone am dull.

As a wave, I float upon the ocean.
I drift, aimless as the wind.

I alone am different from the others;
I drink of the great mother's milk.

21

To achieve the highest virtue,
Remain firmly planted in the Way.
If the Way is beyond comprehension,
How can the people attain its oneness?

Possessing neither form nor substance,
The Way is dark and unfathomable.
Its essence permeates all things in its completeness.
To know this truth, find the centre.

Before time was, the Way is.
Preceding duality,
Its name shall never perish.

How do I know this to be true?
I look inside myself.

22

If you are broken, you shall become whole;
If you are bent, you shall become straight;
If you are empty, you shall become full;
If you are weary, you shall be renewed;
If your desires are few, you shall be satisfied;
If you desire the world, you shall be led astray.

The master embodies this boundless unity
And offers their life as an example to the world.

Free from exhibition, the master shines;
Free from ambition, the master overcomes;
Free from pretension, the master is praised;
Free from identity, the master reflects the soul;
Free from intention, the master succeeds.

When the ancients said,
"To receive everything, give everything up,"
They did not speak in jest.

Offer your life to the Way,
For you receive only what you have given up.

23

One who speaks sparingly
Expresses the spontaneity of nature.
A tempest cannot blow forever
And even the greatest flood abates.
If heaven and earth cannot make these endure,
What hope can we have for our words?

To follow the Way is to become the Way.
Those who seek the Way shall find the Way.
Those who seek virtue shall find virtue.
Those who seek pain shall find pain.

The seeker is free to receive all they find.
Open your heart to the Way
And allow yourself to be found.

24

Who overreaches does not stand firm;
Who oversteps does not stride gracefully;
Who flaunts does not shine;
Who defines themself does not know the self;
Who boasts accumulates no merit;
Those who hold themselves above others cannot endure.

They are as waste and cancer to the Way.
Complete your task, then let it go.

25

Before heaven and earth, all was formless and complete.
Silent and solitary, infinite and invariable,
It exists in all places, in all things.
Ever present, it is the great mother of the universe.

We do not know its name;
Thus, we call it the Way.

If we must speak of it, call it that which is Most High.
It flows through existence, within and without.
Thus, the Way is great, Heaven is great,
Earth is great, and humanity is great.

These are the 4 great powers:
Humans follow the law of Earth;
Earth follows the law of Heaven;
Heaven follows the Way;
The Way follows only itself.

26

Heaviness is the root of lightness;
Stillness is the root of motion.

No matter how far the master travels,
They are always at home.
No matter how glorious the sight,
The master's heart remains unmoved.

To remain the lord of ten thousand chariots,
Take no action lightly.

Act lightly and you shall be uprooted;
If moved to action, you shall lose your position.

27

The skilled traveler leaves no mark of their passing;
The skilled speaker does not stumble;
The skilled counter needs no table.

Though they employ neither bolt nor bar,
The skilled locksmith can secure any gate.

Working with neither cord nor knot,
The skilled rigger's binds cannot be untied.

In this way, the master is a skilled shepherd,
Tending to all who come before them.

Making use of each moment,
The master is completely present.
This is known as Following the Light.

What is a good man, but a bad man's teacher?
What is a bad man, but a good man's lesson?

Fail to honour the teacher,
Fail to learn the lesson,
And you shall be ignorant to your delusion.

This is the essential teaching of the Way.

28

One who knows the Yang, yet preserves the Yin,
Is the ocean which receives all rivers.
Such a one accepts all without prejudice
And follows the Way of Heaven.

Unstained and innocent as a child,
One who knows the light, yet preserves the dark,
Dances in the harmony of the world.
The Way catches their every step
As they return to what is infinite.

One who knows glory, yet preserves humility,
Accepts the world as it is.

The Way of Heaven satisfies all who recognize it;
They return to the simplicity of uncarved wood.

Materials are broken down and shaped into tools,
But the master perceives beyond such divisions
And employs the tools of separation
In the service of reunification.

True creation requires no intervention.

29

You may attempt to seize the world and rule it.
This too shall remain a fruitless endeavour,
For the world cannot be gained through striving.
It remains sacred and cannot be improved.

He who would repair it, does harm to it;
He who would control it, is lost to it.

In all things:
There is a time to lead and a time to follow.
A time for action and a time for rest,
A time for the hard and a time for the soft,
A time to create and a time to destroy.

Thus, the master shuns excess.
They reside in the centre of the circle.

30

One who governs in accordance with the Way
Does not meet their shadow with force of arms,
For violence begets violence untouched by intention.

Where armies once camped, thorns and brambles grow.
In the wake of great battles, fields lie untilled.

The master achieves victory, then shows mercy.
They do not turn rout into slaughter.
They are resolute, without arrogance or pride.
They act from necessity, without thought for honour.

Ill gained glory soon crumbles,
For such action opposes the Way.
Whatever is contrary to the Way
Shall meet an early end.

31

Even the finest weapons are instruments of violence,
Repugnant to all creatures.
Those who follow the Way do not rely on them.

When the master is at peace, they embody the Yin.
When the master is at war, they embody the Yang.

Weapons are not the tools of the wise.
They should only be raised as a last resort.
Peace is far preferable, for blood is the price of victory.
To find joy in triumph is to take pleasure in sorrow.
Whoever drinks from that cup shall not taste satisfaction.

Having won the day,
The lieutenant stands to the left,
The general to the right,
As mourners in a procession.
One who has taken life should weep,
For every battle is a funeral.

32

The Way is ever nameless.
Simple and small, no vessel can contain it.
If only the great and powerful would bow to it,
All of nature would bow to them.
Heaven and Earth would join in harmony;
Sweet rain would fall upon every heart.

All things born of the world can be named.
To have a name is to have an end.
To know the end is to be free of every danger.

The Way is to the world
What the ocean is to the rivers and streams.
It is the completion of all things.

33

To know others is intelligence;
To know the self is true wisdom.
To conquer others is strength;
To conquer the self is true power.

One who is satisfied is rich;
One who perseveres finds success.

Those who remain at the centre shall endure;
Those who embrace death shall never die.

34

The Great Way flows everywhere,
Both to the left and to the right.

All things depend upon it,
Yet it does not withhold its bounty.
Its work complete, it makes no claims.
It clothes and feeds all living beings,
But does not seek to dominate them.

Because it can be found in all places,
It may be called humble.
Because it alone endures after time,
It may be called infinite.

Never striving to be great,
The Way embodies greatness.

35

One who is centred upon the Way
Flows untouched through the world,
In transcendent serenity.

Music and fine food seduce the senses;
True words seem bland and tasteless.

Look, and there is nothing to see;
Listen, and there is nothing to hear.
But make use of it, and it is never ending.

36

To fell a tree, you must first let it grow;
To weaken a rival, you must first make them strong;
To defeat an enemy, you must first raise them up;
To take, you must first have given;
This is the subtle perception of the mystery.

The soft wears down the hard;
The slow catches up to the quick.

As a fish should not be taken from the deep,
Cloak your actions in darkness.

37

The Way does without doing,
Yet nothing is left undone.
If rulers were to keep it,
The kingdom would order itself.
If this order awakens desire,
It shall be satisfied by nameless simplicity.
The uncarved block of wood is free from attachment.
Such liberation is stillness in harmony with the world.

II

The Classic of Virtue

On the appropriate attitude with which to confront the truth

38

The master does not strive for virtue;
Thus, they are able to embody it.
The fool always reaches out for virtue;
Thus, they find none in themself.

The highest virtue does nothing,
Yet nothing is left undone.
The lowest vice is always doing,
Yet never completes its task.

The truly righteous do not act and have no reason to;
They move only when faced with sufficient reason;
The pious act and, if they are not applauded,
They take up arms.

When the Way is lost, only virtue remains;
When virtue is lost, only morality remains;
When morality is lost, only ritual remains.

Ritual is the thin veneer that masks decay;
Prophecy is but a flower petal falling from the Way,
A trap and the beginning of folly.

The master dwells upon the substance, not the surface,
On the fruit, not the flower.
They reject one and accept the other.

39

Before time, all things were as one in the Way.

The heavens attained oneness and became clear;
The earth attained oneness and became serene;
The soul attained oneness and became divine;
The vessel attained oneness and became empty;
The world attained oneness and came to life;
The rulers attained oneness and became just;
These are the virtues of the One.

Without clarity, the sky darkens;
Without serenity, the ground shakes;
Without divinity, the soul wanders;
Without emptiness, the vessel cannot be filled;
Without life, the world will perish;
Without justice, the kingdom falls.

Thus, the essence of virtue is humility,
And the high must be rooted in the low.
When the powerful are alone, hated, and vulnerable,
Are they not closest to humanity?

The greatest honour is free from recognition.
Do not seek the elegance of jade,
Keep to the plainness of stone.

40

The Way proceeds by returning;
Its method is to advance by retreating.
All beings were born of creation,
But creation was born of the Way.

41

For a wise person, to hear of the Way is to embody it.
An average person will acquire it just to lose it again.
When a fool hears of the Way, they will laugh out loud.
If they did not laugh, it would not be the Way.

Thus was it said:
That which is light appears dark;
To move forward we must step back;
The easiest path appears difficult;
The highest virtue appears lowly;
The purest souls appear stained;
The greatest wealth appears modest;
The firmest strength appears frail;
And even perfection is subject to change.

The largest square has no corners;
The deepest vessel cannot be filled;
The loudest noise is silent;
The truest image has no form.

The Way lies hidden from all concepts.
Yet, it is the beginning and end of all things.

42

From the Way came One.
From One came Two.
From Two came Three.
From Three came all of existence.

Every being turns away from the shadow of Yin
While embracing the radiance of Yang,
But between the dance of light and dark,
All things achieve their beauty.

43

That which is soft overcomes that which is hard.
That which is formless exists where there is no space.
The master does without doing and teaches without words.
Students of this Way are few.

44

Should you sacrifice your legacy for health?
Would you sell your life for ever more wealth?
Is it better to gain one or lose the other?

The deeper the love, the sharper the pain;
The more you hold, the more you will lose.

Be content and free from shame;
Show restraint and know no blame.
Thus, the master's life is long.

45

True perfection is a process without completion;
True fullness is the inexhaustible void.

The greatest skill appears simple;
The greatest art appears common;
The greatest wisdom appears foolish.

Movement fends off the chill,
But stillness overcomes heat.
Tranquil in all circumstances,
The master is an example to the world.

46

When a nation follows the Way, horses are bred for the plow;
When a nation turns from the Way, horses are bred for war.

There is no greater lie than fear;
There is no crueller fate than winning your heart's desire.
Give up ambition and attain liberation.

47

Without opening the door, one can know the whole world;
Without seeing the sky, one can know the Way of Heaven.
Thus, the master arrives without ever leaving;
They see without looking, and accomplish without action.

48

The seeker of knowledge gains more each day;
The seeker of the Way gives up more each day.
They abandon doing until they achieve non-action;
When nothing is done, nothing is left undone.

Thus, the master influences by not interfering;
Were they to engage, they would lose their centre.

49

The master's heart is not their own.
The heart of the people beats in their chest.

To those who are good, be good;
To those who are not good, be good also:
That is virtue.
To those who are sincere, be sincere;
To those who are not sincere, be sincere also:
That, too, is virtue.

The master seems to fade into the harmony of the world.
To lay your eyes upon the master
Is to be loved as one of their children.

50

Between birth and death, of every ten:
Three shall follow life, three shall follow death,
And three shall fight to live, only to die,
For sand slips through clenched fingers.

But one who does not cling to life
May travel the land unhindered
And emerge from battle unscathed.
No fang shall find purchase for its poison;
No claw shall find soft flesh to rend.
No weapon could strike such a target;
The taste of death shall never touch their lips.

51

The Way gives life to the universe;
Virtue nurtures it, objects give it shape,
But only when experienced is it complete.

In this manner, all things follow the Way
And express its virtue through their existence.
Such worship is spontaneous as thoughtless breath.
Birth, life, and death are its rituals.

To create without possession,
To act without expectation,
To lead without domination,
This is the hidden virtue of the Way.

52

The world has an origin which may be called the Great Mother.
To know the mother is to know the child.
One who knows the child shall preserve the mother,
And suffer no harm to the end of their days.

Close the gates of your mind
And you shall never be exhausted.
Open yourself to the concerns of the world
And your troubles shall never cease.

To shine in the darkness is enlightenment,
To defend gentleness is strength.
Seek your inner light and return to contentment.
This is known as following eternity.

53

To open one eye is to see the Way.
Next to it, my fears are as smoke.

The Way is easy for all travellers,
Yet still people choose their indirect paths.

When glimmering towers rise over barren fields,
When jeweled swords hang from purple robes,
When feast and famine dine at the same table
And the few impoverish the many,
Such is the time of liars and thieves.

What course could be farther from the Way?

54

One who is rooted upon the Way will never be shaken.
One who embraces the Way will never be forgotten.
They shall benefit their progeny for generations without end.

Cultivate virtue within and the virthe shall be true;
Cultivate virtue within your family and it shall expand;
Cutivate virtue within your village and it shall endure;
Cultivate virtue within your country and it shall spread;
Cultivate virtue in the world and it shall be everywhere.

Thus, see the other as self, all families as your family,
All countries as your country, this world as your world.

How do I know this to be true?
I look within.

55

One who embodies virtue is like an innocent child.
Neither sting, nor fang, nor claw can harm them.

Vulnerable and defenseless, its grip is strong;
Ignorant of lust, its essence is arousal;
Screaming through the night, it never tires;
Such is its harmony with nature.

Knowing this harmony, receive eternity.
Knowing eternity, attain enlightenment.

To hasten life is to invite disaster,
To bend a bough is to risk a break,
To expand unchecked is to become a cancer.

This is contrary to the Way.
Whatever is contrary to the Way
Soon meets its end.

56

One who knows does not speak;
One who speaks does not know.
Close your mouth,
Shut your doors,
Blunt your sharpness,
Loose your knots,
Soften your gaze,
Dissolve into nothingness
And become one with the all.

Neither seduced nor shunned,
Neither helped nor hindered,
Neither decorated nor disgraced,
Become a treasure upon the earth.

57

To govern a nation, be direct;
To wage a war, employ cunning;
To control the world, give up control.

How do I know this?
I observe that:
More prohibitions lead to fewer virtues;
More weapons create greater threats;
More welfare leads to idle dependence;
More laws create more criminals.

Thus, the master says:
Let go of justice and the people become honest;
Let go of worry and the people care for themselves;
Let go of striving and the people prosper;
Let go of desire for the good
And the good becomes common.

58

When a ruler is tolerant, the people are lawful;
When a ruler is strict, the people are rebellious.
Good fortune and woe rest on the toss of a coin;
No one can predict their fate.

In time, the normal becomes strange
And that which is fair becomes foul.
This is the source of all confusion.

Thus, the master is sharp, but does not cut;
Is straight, but not rigid;
Is radiant, but not blinding;
Is content, and does not impose their will.

59

In governing people and in serving heaven,
Nothing surpasses moderation.

To moderate the self is to submit to the Way;
To submit to the Way is to accumulate merit;
To accumulate merit is to overcome limitation;
To overcome limitation is to open your eyes.

Only one who can see is fit to rule,
For they shall guard the country as their own mother.
Under such care, the nation endures.

These are the deep roots of the oldest trees.

60

Governing a nation is like frying a small fish…

Trust in the Way and evil shall not touch it.
Though evil is abundant, it can do no harm.
Finding no opponent, evil defeats itself.

…Too much interference ruins the dish.

61

A great state is like the ocean into which all rivers flow.
The essence of Yin, it receives the world.

The feminine overcomes the masculine through stillness,
By accepting the masculine when it returns to its origin.

Thus, by humbling itself,
The large nation invites loyalty.
Likewise, by humbling itself,
The small nation invites patronage.

One wins by becoming modest;
The other wins by remaining modest.
A great state desires to unite and protect;
A great vassal desires to serve and support.

All are blessed by cultivating humility.

62

The Way is an altar to the universe;
It is a good man's treasure and a bad man's refuge.

Fine words may purchase influence
And honourable deeds may purchase rank,
Even when one wanders from virtue.

When the Light of Heaven assumes the throne,
Let others offer icons of power and wealth.
None are as highly esteemed
As one who bears only the Way.

Why did the ancients kneel before the Way?
Was it not said:
In the Way, those who seek shall find
And those who sin shall be forgiven?
In this way, it is the jewel of creation.

63

WEI WU WEI
SHI WU SHI
WEI WU WEI

See the low as the high
And the few as the many.
Meet hostility with kindness.

The master overcomes the difficult while it is easy
And accomplishes the great by attending to the small.

Thus, it is because the master does not attempt great things
That they are able to accomplish them.

Promises made in haste are broken hastily;
Trust in an easy journey will ensure its difficulty.
The master treats each moment with equal care
And avoids all dangers.

64

When rooted, it is easy to nourish;
When recent, it is easy to correct;
When brittle, it is easy to break;
When small, it is easy to crush.

Address problems before they arise;
Establish order while there is yet peace.

The broadest tree emerged from a single seed;
The tallest tower has a foundation of dirt;
A journey of a thousand leagues begins with a single step.

Try and you shall fail;
Seize and you shall lose.
The master does by not doing and cannot fail;
Their hands are empty, so they embrace the world.

Failure so often lies at the doorway to success.
View the end as the same as the beginning
And every success is assured.

Therefore, the master desires only freedom from desire
And does not value precious goods.
They have learned not to learn;
They redeem the sins of the world.

By neither presuming to interfere
Nor enforcing their will,
The master assists every soul
As they return to the self.

65

The ancient masters of the Way
Did not seek to impart wisdom,
But helped the people realize their own ignorance.
Those who think they know are difficult to govern.

One who knows walks upon the path of folly;
One who knows only that they do not know
Is a blessing to the world.

These two principles govern the universe,
For they partake of the deepest virtues.
Such virtue is so sublimely limitless
That it draws all things back to source
And attains oneness with them.

66

Every river flows to the sea
Because it lies beneath them.

Thus, one who would rule must raise the people high,
And one who would lead the people must follow them.

The master:
Stands above the people, but does not crush them;
Stands in front of the people, but does not obstruct them;
Is exalted by the people, but does not exhaust them.

Resisting no one, no one resists the master.

67

Those who know the Way
Say it is infinite, but appears empty.
It is only because the Way is infinite
That it appears to be empty.
If it did not appear empty,
It would fade into nothingness.

Those who know the Way
Cherish three treasures:
Love, moderation, and humility.
With love, your heart can be courageous;
With moderation, you are free to accept what comes;
With humility, the whole world follows your example.

Those who know the Way
Understand that courage without love,
Liberty without moderation,
Power without humility,
Are sure paths to destruction.

Fight in the name of these treasures and victory is assured;
Make these treasures your shield and safety is guaranteed.
Heaven protects all who show such compassion.

68

The ideal soldier is not anxious;
The ideal general cannot be provoked;
The ideal lord is not vengeful;
The ideal minister is not proud.

This is the virtue of non-resistance.
By accepting the truth of the world,
One may dance in the flow of heaven.

69

Among Strategists, there is a saying:
I dare not play the host, but rather be the guest;
I dare not advance an inch, but rather retreat a yard.

This is known as
Maneuver without movement,
War without battle,
Conflict without weapons,
Vigilance without an enemy.

All war is total war.
Underestimate your opponent
And all you hold dear shall be taken.

When armies clash,
The mournful shall be victorious.

70

These words are easy to understand and easy to practice,
Yet none are able to.
These words are older than the world.

Because we do not know ourselves,
The people cannot know these words.
Those who appreciate these words are rare,
But those who follow them are treasured.

The master's roughspun tunic
Hides precious jade beneath.

71

To know that we do not know is true knowledge;
To think we know when we do not is a disease.
One must identify a cancer before it can be removed.
Thus, the master works to exorcise their own ignorance
And remain free from all afflictions.

72

Without awe for the awesome,
We are at the mercy of the awful.
If you do not restrict those under your care,
They will not be crushed by the weight of your rule.
Thus, the master knows, but does not say;
Their love requires no decoration.

They seek within and discover without.

73

Reckless courage leads to death;
Disciplined courage may prevent it.
One appears superior to the other,
But the hands that weave our fate are blind.
Not even the master can explain it.

The Way of Heaven:
Overcomes without opposing;
Communicates without speaking;
Arrives without leaving;
Accomplishes without striving.

The net of Heaven is cast so wide
That all things are caught within it.

74

One who does not fear death
Cannot be threatened into obedience.
Those who lives in fear of execution
Might be arrested and murdered.
But who would dare?

There is One who presides over death.
To kill in their stead would be
To take the place of the master carpenter.
Few may handle the master's tools
Without drawing their own blood.

75

Why do the people starve?
Their rulers levy too much in taxes.
Why do the people rebel?
Their rulers impose upon their lives.
Why do the people fear death?
They cling too tightly to life.

It is better to live your life
Than to spend your time preserving it.

76

Born, we are soft and supple;
Dead, we are stiff and hard.
In Spring, all are tender and delicate;
In Winter, all are dried and withered.

One who is rigid is a disciple of death;
One who is yielding is an acolyte of life.

An army that cannot yield will be destroyed.
A tree that cannot bend will break and fall.
In the end, the proud shall be humbled
And the humble shall stand proud.

77

The Way of Heaven is like stringing a bow;
The high is pulled down; the low is raised up.
It removes excess and satisfies deficiency.

The Way of Heaven is to take from abundance
To fill the cups of wanting.
The Way of Man is to take from the hands of poverty
To fill the appetite of gluttony.

Who can serve the world without thought for the self?
Only one who follows the Way.

The master acts without expectation.
They achieve a goal and move on to the next,
Taking no credit for their accomplishment.

78

Nothing in the world is as soft and yielding as water,
Yet nothing else can carve a valley through the mountains.

> The weak overcomes the strong;
> The soft overcomes the hard.
> All can understand this,
> But none can achieve it.

> The master has said,
> One who takes up the shame of the nation
> Is beloved by the spirit of the land.
> And one who takes up the suffering of the nation
> Shall be hailed as sovereign under Heaven.

Truth is often cloaked in paradox.

79

When old enemies are reconciled
The shadow of resentment remains.
Who benefits from this?

The master pays the debts he owes
And forgives the debts owed to them.

One possessing virtue honours their word;
One lacking virtue demands compensation.

The Way of Heaven is impartial in its love;
It always accumulates to that which is good.

80

An ideal nation should be small, its people few.

Though they have machines by the hundred,
They do not use them;
Though they are mindful of death,
They do not flee from it;
Though they have all manner of vehicles,
They have no destination to drive them;
Though they have armour and weapons,
They have no battlefield to deploy them.

Let the people return to simplicity.
Let them delight in fresh food,
Find their rough clothes beautiful,
See their modest homes as castles,
And rejoice in their everyday bliss.

There should be a neighbouring state within sight.
Though its dogs and fowl can be heard,
The people will meet a long life's end
Not having ever gone to visit.

81

True words are not beautiful;
Beautiful words are not true.
Those who are wise do not argue;
Those who argue are not wise.

The master holds no possessions.
The more they do for others,
The greater their fortune;
The more they give to others,
The richer they become.

The Way benefits all under Heaven.
The master does without doing
And accomplishes without effort.

Honoured Translators

A C GRAHAM
ALEISTER CROWLEY
ARTHUR WALEY
ALAN WATTS
CH'U TA-KAO
DARRELL LAU
DEREK LIN
EDWARD HERBERT
GIA-FU FENG & JANE ENGLISH
ISABELLA MEARS
JAMES LEGGE
JOHN BLOFIELD
JOHN C H WU
JOHN CHALMERS
LIONEL GILES
R. JOSEPH OWLES
ROBERT ENO
ROBERT HENRICKS
ROGER AMES & DAVID HALL
RICHARD WILLHELM
S. MITCHELL
STEFAN STENUDD
STEPHEN ADDISS & STANLEY LOMBARDO
TIM CHILCOTT

**URSULA K LE GUIN
WING-TSIT CHAN**

Also by Nicholas [Wong Lai Beng]

It is my goal to complete a book each year on the Spring equinox. Each work is the product of ideas and concepts received by this imperfect vessel. Having started in the year 2020, An Interpretation of the Way is the second book in the series.

The Way of Dying

A short collection of 23 poetic verses regarding the relationship between Truth, Life, and Love as perceived through the penetrating eyes of Death.

www.ingramcontent.com/pod-product-compliance
Lightning Source LLC
Chambersburg PA
CBHW072206100526
44589CB00015B/2388